CREOLE MÉTISSE OF FRENCH CANADA, ME

D1248787

Creole Métisse of French Canada, me © Sharron Proulx-Turner 2018

Published by Kegedonce Press
11 Park Road
Neyaashiinigmiing, Ontario N0H 2T0
www.kegedonce.com
Administration Office/Book Orders
P.O. Box 517 - Owen Sound ON - N4K 5R1

Printed in Canada by Ball Media
Cover Design: Eric Abram
Design: Eric Abram

Library and Archives Canada Cataloguing in Publication

Proulx-Turner, Sharron, author
    Creole Métisse of French Canada, me / Sharron
Proulx-Turner.

Poems.
ISBN 978-1-928120-10-0 (softcover)

    I. Title.

PS8581.R68983C74 2017   C811'.6   C2017-903965-2

Sales and Distribution – http://www.lpg.ca/LitDistco:

For Customer Service/Orders
Tel 1–800–591–6250 Fax 1–800–591–6251
100 Armstrong Ave. Georgetown, ON L7G 5S4
Email orders@litdistco.ca
We acknowledge the support of the Canada Council for the Arts which last year
invested
$20.1 million in writing and publishing throughout Canada.

THE CANADA COUNCIL | LE CONSEIL DES ARTS
FOR THE ARTS | DU CANADA
SINCE 1957 | DEPUIS 1957

We would like to acknowledge funding support from the Ontario Arts Council, an
agency of the Government of Ontario.

ONTARIO ARTS COUNCIL
CONSEIL DES ARTS DE L'ONTARIO
50 YEARS OF ONTARIO GOVERNMENT SUPPORT OF THE ARTS
50 ANS DE SOUTIEN DU GOUVERNEMENT DE L'ONTARIO AUX ARTS

for Sharron Marguerite Proulx-Turner

I watch the snow fall outside my bedroom window,
a blank page in front of me,
when I should be singing

Our dear mentor, friend, aunty, mother, Nokomis. The months have passed since last November when you said you would like to take us all with you, on your journey, that letting go was the hardest part. I have known you for what feels like forever, since your long silver hair was coiffed stylishly short, grew long into a braid or loose around your face over the years, and then disappeared with your treatments, only to return those past few weeks, in short curls and waves. Perhaps it was a vanity of yours that you covered your head with a cap, a hat, a fedora, a sparkly cancer scarf, and that we found our faces so often reflected back to us in your sunglasses.

I have witnessed your loves and lonelinesses, triumph and despair. I have witnessed the growth of your children into almost middle-age. And your grandchildren grow, too, some already into teens and adulthood. If there is a place of meeting where you are now, I hope it is a place of love and joy, of talk, feasting and peace. And a quiet place to write, by a river.

You were often a person of few words, deliberate in your speech, but also direct, a teller of story-truths, even when they were not always welcome. You were gifted with the ability to challenge us with love, a difficult gift to learn and to craft. I learned so much about truth and how to tell it, from you, about teaching, writing, friendship, advocacy. So many of us still struggling with the demands of this world we still inhabit have learned from your spirit, gentleness, and clarity, and how tenaciously and courageously you worked for all of these, not just for yourself but for others. We knew, at times, how often you felt your courage failed you when it didn't always show, particularly in the last year of your life, and with illness. You said, so often, how essential it was for you to write about that experience, the strangeness of living with cancer, facing the certainty of death.

I am so sorry that this eluded you in the end. But with that same tenacity, you completed this book, and charged many of us with making sure it saw the light of day.

You wrote not long ago, "If you can talk you can sing, and if you can sing, you can write." And you leave such a legacy of writing: your books of poetic prose, which I have, like others, read again in the past while. They amaze me still, whether they were dedication poems to your friends and family in the book she is reading her blanket with her hands; the history and voice of your ancestors in she walks for days/ inside a thousand eyes: a two-spirit story; the celebration of the aunties' and your own stories and day-to-day wisdom in what the auntys say, beckylane's searing story-memoir where the rivers join; the wonderful collection of poetic storytelling in the trees are still bending south, or your collaboration with Beverly Little Thunder in One Bead At A Time. Your passion for writing saw you through to the end of editing this, perhaps your final book.

Writers write for many reasons, but writing itself was both joy and survival for you and a gift to your communities, an investment in and proof of their resilience as well as yours. Someone said of your writing, especially of your titles, that they were like incantations or prayers, and I know of no other writer so gifted, even in your regular morning e-mails, at capturing the spirit of a moment with such mystical, meditative precision, wonder and, of course, humour.

In the end, we learned to talk with you instead, to keep words in memory, so that final gift you gave us was another one of relationship and words: as we spoke with you, tended to your needs (and ours), we also met and re-met people who were part of your life, touched in so many ways by theirs: waves and ripples formerly concentric met in your small room with its picture window at Rosedale Hospice. Those meetings were full of laughter, and reminiscence, food, tea and coffee, lots of water, questions, tears, photos, singing, smudging, drumming: figuring out the web of connections and relations, watching as new ones developed, especially with your caregivers who in their short time with you, were so deeply affected by your remarkable presence. And much silence. And you, in those 25 years gave me such lasting gifts, not just of your very self, but of relationship with your amazing family. To the end, you exhorted me and others to write, to sing for myself and for a wider world.

I write this in the way that you wrote your dedication poems, because, if I didn't, all I would do is write about your life intertwined with mine and with those of us still here. I would inhabit my grief and the blankness of the page. My tears are less frequent now, and I find myself amazed still, and always thankful that you are still so present to me. To hear you sing was an amazing experience. You sang for the hospice folks. You sang for your children. You kept singing. Your friend Richard van Camp tells us that you must be now leading a round dance. His words for you: Dance you sweet Aunty of Light. Dance and sing. You are free. You will always be honoured for your courage, your bravery, your grace. Mahsi cho for your life as ceremony and mahsi cho for reminding us all to have more fun, to make time for feasting and to host the ceremonies that the world needs and deserves.

Letting go was the hardest part for you, you said. And it is for us as well, because we have chosen to stay behind. And part of our ongoing grief is to recognize how difficult it can be, living life, to remember what you said to us over and over again in those last few weeks, that "love is all there is". You wagged your finger at one of those moments and said "and I don't mean like The Beatles". Indeed, my friend: I hope you are still around to remind us how this works in all of its complexity, day-to-day, for us scaredy-cats still hanging around here.

I will end by turning to acknowledge those of you without whom this book would never have happened: Barb, Graham, Harold, Alicia, Aimée, Willow, Jessinia, Mazie-Anna, and Ariston were meaning and world to Sharron. To the wide circle of family and friends—so many—who sustained her through her last months, with your presence, words, support and guidance: to Paul and Connie Morin, especially.

To those of you who took the time with this manuscript, I am certain Sharron would express her heartfelt gratitude, even if she'd have made different decisions! She was especially thankful to Susan Briscoe for her amazing editorial skill with this work as it developed. To Weyman Chan, thank-you for taking on the task of editing the final manuscript of one of your dearest friends and for reading poetry to her into the wee hours. To those of you at Kegedonce, a million thanks—to Renée and Patricia, and especially Kateri for your friendship and vision and for ensuring that this project that Sharron worked on through incredible pain and with great fortitude is finally published. And to all of you for your patience with this gaggle of grieving family and friends.

To Sharron's family. Your mama and Nokomis and sister Sharron is singing for you. To Sharron, we dedicate this to you with love.

Aruna Srivastava, September 2017

Contents

The nut house

my great grandfather, napoleon proulx, had two sons
named reg. one was born with two hearts. lived till he
was four years old. he was bipolar, napoleon proulx.
sometimes he'd be committed to the psych ward at the
royal hospital in ottawa because he was heard singing
to his late twin boys. soon as he got there he'd wrap
himself up in his blue capote and take off back home on
foot. once there he'd play the fiddle for his boys. under
the bird house in the back yard. that bird house was as
long as the oaks all around the house were tall. dozens
of swallows living inside, side-by-side, like the métis.

he told my grandmother something once, napoleon
proulx, his voice quiet and musical. she was seven
years old at the time. kept them as her own, those
words. even today I sing out his song like a warm and
watery two-step, hearts beating to the rhythms of the
ottawa's south and eastward flow:
there are days when I feel
so close to my métis heart
I hear my blood move through my chest
across my temples my métis blood
breathes with me
that slow and steady heat
our métis hearts beat
       beat
    beating to the rhythms
of my little twin boys

napoleon proulx liked to look out from where the ottawa meets the rideau, the old highways of birch bark canoes filled with bare-thighed métis men. their woolen métis caps, even at summer's height, their heads like the scarlet beebalm blossoms bursting through the blues and greens along the shores. deer skin leggings, breech cloths, moccasins. short shirts. hazelnut pipes. sashes and beaded bags. and fiddles. always the fiddles. that's how we won the ladies, he used to say. not with big houses or ribbons or cloth. played the violin till dawn.

at portage or change of direction in the big birch bark canoes, us métis we marked our routes with mai. not mai like the month, but mai concerning trees––spruces and pines. removed their lower limbs. stood out like green-skirted ladies those mai. opened up the forest sun. a fine and welcome sight.

napoleon proulx called his day the beginnings of the great collapse. the french. the spanish and the portuguese. the english. he would laugh, his shoulders up and down, up and down, his mouth open like the letter o. our mixed families? we couldn't be frenchified so the government raided poorhouses in paris, lyon, rouen, dieppe. whiten up québec with soft white ladies was their plan. called their ladies chattel the french did. cattle. fined the fathers when their daughters wouldn't marry and made widows remarry before their late mates were even in the ground, their tears like water pooling around the trunks of maples and pines.

they lumbered the land here, our ancestors did. travelled the great waters when trees were all you could see. maples, oaks, elms, poplars, birches, spruces, sumac, pines. us métis were illegal in this land for hundreds of years. shot and killed on sight. the free people. not defined nor bound to any

government. the frenchman was slow to learn about
life on this land. like how to steer and land and load
a canoe, how to live with the bugs. how to make and
walk on snowshoes, how to embrace the cold. basic
skills. us métis, we found a way to marry the ways of
our ancestors on both sides, trade freely with our kin.
our relatives they came from all over in those early
days. wore moccasins and recherche ruffled shirts.
blue pantaloons, too. leggings. a capote and a red
métis sash. long hair. fine tattoos and embroidery. at
least one of them carried the fiddle. keeps us
happy that. makes remembering our way.

House fire

the métis are not originally from the north west but have taken root on the banks of the saint laurence (and the ottawa).

–étienne rivard

in 1900 a fire raged across the bridge from hull into ottawa, billowed down booth street. stopped by the wetlands that now house carleton university. my great grandfather, napoleon proulx, lived on booth street. suspended his parents in their well to escape the fire. sprinted up the road, kitchen table upside down on his head. piled there, precious photos. a family heirloom gingerbread clock. firebag. a métis sash. a violin.

as far back as anyone knows, the violin has been a part of métis dress. too expensive to buy or trade, us métis learned to make our own fiddles from maple and birch. the more a fiddle's played, the higher its value. still today. fiddles come from europe, but the music, the rhythms, the tempo, the beat, the dances, are distinctly indigenous. fiddle playing is learned through oral teachings. the sound post has a spirit––the wood is alive. like the drum, like the languages, the fiddle surrounds a room with movement and settles in the bone.

in english, the instrument, the fiddle itself is a noun.
an inanimate object. english is noun-driven, compelled
by inanimate objects. rigid and unyielding to speakers
of first peoples' tongues when it comes to expressing
movement, growth, life. the solution for some métis?
michif. nouns are french and english. verb structures
cree, ojibwe. métis english. québecois french. both with
their heavy cree cadence. a reader once commented on
my writing in an audience. said she heard me speak
in english and french. and she heard a third language.
what is that language, she wanted to know? I thanked
her for hearing a third language. the lady went on to
say she's from jamaica and over there they're told they
don't speak english. and they don't, she said. they call
their language creole, a mix.

the sash with its mix of colours and weaves, is a
noun. us métis, we adopted the sash from our eastern
woodland relatives. the first to weave and wear them.
before goat's wool was introduced, the woodland
peoples used plant fibres. even the french started
wearing sashes, but much later, during the lower
canada uprisings. sashes are not from europe as many
believe, though wool is. when wool was introduced,
sashes were made from very fine goat's wool, waxed
and re-twisted. so close they were often water-resistant.
the finest sashes—fibre or wool—took two hundred
hours to make. métis wore the sash under their coats.
when they weren't wrapped around the waist two
or three times, sashes were used as rope, tumplines,
bridles, saddle blankets, wash cloths, towels, first aid,
emergency sewing kits, pockets, water carriers.

firebag is a noun. flint and steel carriers. black wool
stroud. flowered beadwork. the firebag that was to be
handed down to my great grandfather fell from the
upturned table. the fiddle, too. burned. hot, blistering

fire. another noun. how could a noun incinerate two-thirds of hull and a fifth of ottawa in 1900? level the railway line? put fifteen thousand people in tent cities? fed by strong winds and staggering stacks of timber-- the slaughter of great forests that lined the ottawa river's edge. the timber combusted, throwing the fire skyward and down the city streets.

the heinous loss of lives, not just humans. all the ancestors who shared that land from time immemorial. the great forests. the animals. the waters. the birds. the rocks. the insects. the earth. their homes. all nouns. all inanimate. all objects.

Sweeping the house

between the 17th and 19th centuries, a canadian nation was formed that originated exclusively with the creoles of french america. this nation seems to have relinquished its original name, and in this last quarter of the 20th century, it now refers to itself as the québecois people.

–jean morisset

my aunty used to say, when québec wakes up there'll be six million more indians. simple logic or history lesson, depending on the view. she was a history buff, my aunty. not the book kind of learning so much as oral learning that teaches about how québec is the single largest mixed-blood nation in canada. for generations, law after law after law after law passed against the free mixedblood people of québec. the only way to stay alive was to stay clear of the black robes. unlike the clergy, the old québec maps don't lie. my aunty showed me a map dated 1758. just as a cree cadence on top of pure france french created the full, ever-fluid creole of french canada, so aunty's map pointed to an island in new brunswick, ile de métisse. a town called mitis where the rivière mitis hits the st. laurent.

coureurs de bois, creole du canada, canadiens, canadians, marchands chasseurs, cajuns, boheme, engagés, habitants, bois brulé, mozo, métis.

red river métis didn't just pop out of the land like maize and sage. this is where aunty always threw up her hands. métis and sage––métissage she might say today. then those soft hands down to her belly every time she reminded us it all started nine months after the first europeans landed on these shores. the euskaldunak, the basque. thousands of mixed blood along with the french mixed bloods. even had their own mixed tongue, the euskaldunak. too, nine months after the first french landed, a new, unique culture began. the french mixed-bloods, the métis, who established tadoussac in 1599.

anglais, bembenyiik, boschlopers, opitow-coosan, brulé, canayen, freemen, half-men, gens de libre, natives, half-caste, englishman, country-born.

tadoussac. one of the first métis settlements that made it to the map. and, yes, there were métis uprisings before batoche, she'd puff all up then, aunty would. several. you think we were asleep before our relatives made the carts on the plains? before frog lake and fish creek? in the history books, uprisings were men's work. but us métis, we don't act alone. women and men, indians and métis? we were one and the same. worked together since way back before the early 1600s when métis negotiated treaties alongside the other nations. fought beside our maliseet and mi'kmaw relatives. same for later on with the royal proclamation. aunty would laugh, everyone knows that date. 1763. no white man allowed to settle west of the appalachians at the time. lasted for the blink of an eye, but we remember those glory days, us métis. aunty would start to relax when she reached this point in her story, her face filled with joy. what folks nowadays don't seem to remember? in all the documents that pre-date our mixed-blood relative mr. duncan campbell scott and his treaties and poems? métis and indians are one and the same.

pontiac's leadership in the three-year rebellion, 1763-66? his was a prophetic call. the ottawa, kickapoo, wyandot. peoria, ojibwe, miami, potawatomi, the wea, the métis. and more. a united force. their success renowned, even today. that one made the white man's history books. not the way we would of told it, but at least there's a picture of an indian who doesn't look like he just popped out of a white man's painting from that era. she'd pause, laugher in her voice, like paul rubens' saturn devouring his son. the métis were gathering up to defend the land around the sault. long before the birth of charles de langlade and the leadership this great métis man provided around the great lakes. led a powerful mixed-blood, indian troop himself. many more women and men––impossible to name here–– led the métis peoples to our homes.

home guard cree, huskies, livyers, pedlars, rupertslanders, ootipayimsowak, malouidit, mustee, muktum, chicot, pork eaters, vagabonds, vagrants, bungi, michif.

all these words used for naming us métis––all from outsiders. throughout the world there's a habit of outside naming, outside framing. no different for us métis. our names come from elsewhere. our history in the school books, too. comes from the white man. then the feds started to keep us out of the treaties. too many of us. scared them. and today? fear brews up and boils. government busts us up province by province. always has. want to make us believe this one or that one's not really one of us. aunty is a prophet, as many of the old elders like her are today. cautions us, the government wants to make us believe our own kids are not métis, our own grandkids for seven generations. wants to make us forget who we are. we're more than just carts and fiddles. sashes and the

red river jig. more than just puffy square dancers'
skirts and starched ribbon shirts.

promyshlennki, chicot, apeytogosan, peddler,
home indian, non-status indian, habitant, scots,
labradorian, vagabonds, vagrants, bungi, mitcheef,
breed, prairie nigger.

since time immemorial, our ancestors did not fight just
for themselves. they fought for us. that's who we are.
we look ahead seven generations with every breath.
we breathe the same air as that first baby métis. we
live all over the darn place. plain and simple. we're in
a time of great need. we have got to come together. it.
is. up. to. us. each one of us is a seventh generation.
and us seventh generationers? we have got to get a
move on. change doesn't come in a few hours, or even
in a few days. no internet is going to bring about real
rock solid change. prayer. political activism. the arts.
that's our way. so don't take no short cuts, says aunty.
write. paint. dance. perform. raise up those voices. lift
up those drums, those sacred pipes. pray with every
breath of every day. métis carts came centuries after the
first métis rebellion. not one piece of metal was used
on a métis cart. the squeak and squeal of the wooden
wheels could be heard for miles. listen. remember. a
century is only a spoke in a wheel. you have got to keep
witnessing, my girl, is what my aunty would say. you
gotta never give up.

The longhouse

there are people who will try to hurt you because of the good they see in you, needing that good for themselves. they'll try to beat it out of you. when you come to know that, don't become like those people.

−evelyn t.r. boyce

I dream of a large room, where the wind blowing indoors doesn't seem out of the ordinary. though the room is full of people, I feel alone, lonely for a friend. my childhood home was like that, like I didn't belong, with my mom stretching out a silence I wasn't meant to break. the silence concerned me, mom teaching the older ones, the younger ones the dangers of me. my biggest flaw was I was too nice, too kind. not natural, my mom would say. born evil, that one. watch your back.

in dreamworld there are mirrors up above in the large room. I can see myself and each strand of my hair contains volumes of knowledge forming along the waves. the wind picks up words, like dust from my hands, my skin, my hair––swirling them into a tiny twister whose point reaches into my left eye. and rather than close my eyes, I hold them open to the harshness of those words, the blinding sting that opens a doorway to the past.

I'm reminded of a story I heard some years ago, where trickster loses her eyes after juggling them for too long—even though she's warned this will happen—and her eyes don't return. she starts to go around with flowers in her empty sockets, telling the people she encounters how special her eyes are and how she can see things no one else can see. person after person offers to trade one eye for one of hers, until, one day, a girl offers to trade both her eyes for these special eyes that can see things no one else can see. when the trade is made, the girl is left without sight.

but the girl knows that darkness holds stories and songs of great power, and when she recounts them in her mind, they shift her thoughts away from herself to the voices of the women who came before her.

she dreams about her grandmother. in the dream, she's a teen and there are other kids, lots of them, maybe sisters and brothers and cousins. her grandmother has them all helping to clear out a canoe, a very, very long canoe that's large enough for an extended family. the canoe is made from bark, not from wood. because she's the oldest, her grandmother asks her to go out with the canoe and retrieve a medicine from the bottom of the water. the water is dark and murky. it takes several dives before the girl is able to pull up the medicine for her grandmother. she knows this is a powerful healing medicine. when she reaches the surface after her final dive and opens her eyes, she's in a circle of women.

she goes around the circle shaking the women's hands, introducing herself. she reaches her mother, surprised she's there. when they shake hands, they laugh and shake hands again. her mother's hand feels like her own hand, like she's shaking her own hand. her mother's talking and the girl leans down to hear what her mother is saying, her left ear to her mother's mouth. her mother makes a joke in her ear. the girl tells a joke back. wakes herself up laughing.

The foster house

when the "family fire" is not kept burning, our whole social order begins to decay and fall into disorder.

—13 indigenous grandmothers

a fire in my apartment building. had to live in a hotel for three months. all my stuff was professionally cleaned and boxed and labeled. a long-time friend offered to buy me a place of my own. I was speechless. felt like a child, filled with glee and hope, love and gratitude. it will take a month or two, she said, but don't unpack your boxes. don't settle back in. I waited. a while longer, she said. after a year, I started to name the boxes after my late ancestors. big red letters: exilda, marguerite, josephte. rosina, jeanne d'arc, anna, germaine. one for each passing month. a while longer, she said. I started to feel like I was trying to hold back one of those floating islands on the headwaters in peachland, bc. twenty months I waited, cupboards and closets and book shelves still bare. boxes lining the floors, the walls, spilling out of the halls, musty and discoloured now by soot and dust from the highway not six metres away. piled and named, my ancestors framed my hope with disappointment and something like a festering self-blame.

like that sick feeling when I was a child and my mom
would strip me down for enemas. that stick thing hurt
so bad so far up a burst of hot pain. week after week
after month after year sitting there on that bucket.
out there in the open, counting the big white and
black tiles on the floor. trying to hold still so quiet so
perfectly still. words burned onto the sides of my head
my ears my cheeks, a flat, open palm.

don't get thrown off the bucket blow after blow after
blow. meant cleaning up the floor. scrubbing. hands
and knees and soap and poop and blood all over
coming down all around.

childhood trauma is hard to read. stops me from
writing, more memories flooding in. much, much
worse. from my dad. from a shrink doctor man. from
many strange women and men. life's building blocks.

almost every childhood day that I remember my mom
would draw a picture of a woman. just her head. forties
hairdo. a simple line drawing, but there was beauty
hidden there, a peace and a calmness that showed great
talent. not that I knew that then. I asked her if that
lady was her and her answer was always the same. we
are made up of memory she would say. we've survived
the brutality. we'll survive the rest. I never saw the
best parts of my mom because she showed me only
the broken parts. some experiences are so heinous
they change your dna, she would say. the way we were
treated was just plain inhumane.

copied what she learned when she was young. enemas.
beatings. confinement. overworking her babies' little
bodies. ate at her belly, her lungs, her brain. my mom
was fostered out––as it was called by the child welfare
system. her family ripped apart during the war years, a
ruse to herd métis and non-status children into white

people's homes. farm slaves. kill the métis within the child. my mom never talked about it to me, maybe because she married her final foster mother's brother.

but others in her family talked. the ones who spent their whole growing up lives trapped there in my dad's sister's house. couldn't go past grade six. couldn't stay awake in school. exhausted. hungry. forced to wash fly poop out of the cracks in the massive white tongue and groove kitchen walls. with a toothbrush. hand pressed down on the red hot stove. left a speck of fly poop. not fast enough with the chores. decomposing chicken tied around the neck like jewellery for days. to teach a lesson. roped to a chair and lowered in a well day and night and day and night. for sport. prepared the large family meals

 then fed the pig scraps on rusted tin pans then sent out to feed the pigs. bed a wooden trunk, wool blanket for a sheet. no top blanket. no pillow. to be caught covering with that rough, worn wool brought on beatings and worse. so much worse.

in my mid-thirties I studied fine arts. my mom had already died. I loved to draw, with pencil and with chalk. when assigned to compose a bestial self-portrait, I drew something cold. visceral. turned me inside out. it was simple enough, a being that was part cat, part androgynous human. what hit me was the composition, the squatted creature looking out from a cement cage, unable to move. shook loose memory, pulled at time. last drawing I did for more than twenty years. I couldn't sort out my feelings, escaped now in lines on a page.

it was only much later that I saw something hidden inside that empty feline stare. just as my mom's lady with her glassy eyes concealed a hopeful dream, that cat's haunting vertical stare filled a room with the wisdom of desire. a distant star, holding everything, even my heart. knowing every thought I'd ever had, every feeling. when my eyes stray skyward now, I see her, my mom, even in the day. her drawing, my drawing layered on top of hers. I see her in the trees in the night, in my grandchildren's tiny hands. I hear her hearing me. and I miss her, oh how I miss her. the life I have been given is hers. I asked her to come and she came, showing me the whole of something I do not understand. and this is all there is, all there will be, until I know.

The safehouse

*medical experimentation in america in the 1950s and '60s
illustrates the chilling legacy of negative eugenics–– the
sickening imperative to prevent the survival and reproduction
of the least fit––and the push by the 20th- century medical
establishment to find cures and treatments using children as
human guinea pigs.*

**–jill marsal on, against their will: the secret history of
medical experimentation on children in cold war america**

first day of school I walked with my head down. I
was shy. withdrawn. already stoop-shouldered. I still
sucked a soother and I felt exposed wearing a dress. I
found that I liked school much more than home, but
I had dyslexia and a speech disorder and back in the
fifties I was considered mute and slow. retarded. so I
was tested. I guess I passed. an old lady came to help me
learn, skills I still use today. I felt a sense of belonging
to that place, school. my safehouse.

from early on until well into my thirties I had two
recurring nightmares. in one, I was forced to stand
in front of a large gathering of military men who
were all dressed in formal summer wear. I was small.
six? seven? still had some baby teeth. the heat was
welcoming and the sky a dry-spell sky, a rare deep blue.

no haze. the men sat around tables, in the shape of a
rectangle with one short end open, shaded by army
tents. at the opening, a doctor man had me by a chain,
hooked to a collar around my neck. he

pulled at me like a dog. hard. called me pig and hog. but
mostly he called me lucky. I was his lucky he would
say. his lucky charm. made me carry a round brown
cooler, bulky and heavy for me. inside the cooler there
were strips of rotting raw meat. the doctor man was
handsome. clean. smelled good. early fifties. cropped
straight auburn hair. same tallness as my dad. the
doctor man talked for a long time to the men there. he
talked about me. voice like music. told them I would do
anything he said. told me to open the cooler and set the
lid aside. told me to tell him I love him. I shook my head,
no. told me again. no. yanked at the collar. no. held me
up in the air by my neck by the chain, my feet dangling,
his spit his face in mine. put his other big hand into the
thermos and shoved a handful of rank meat into my
mouth. I couldn't breathe. gagging. no air. woke up.

in grad school I told this nightmare to a friend. he was
thoroughly undone. shocked, not just by the nightmare
itself he said, but by the language used by the man. he
asked had I ever read beckett? the playwright? I told
him, no. you have to read waiting for godot, he said. it's
going to blow your mind. and it did. there's a slave in
the play named lucky, with a rope tied round his chafed
neck. he's controlled by another character who hauls
him around, yanks at the rope. calls him hog and pig.
unless told otherwise, lucky holds the master's coat
and a picnic basket, a suitcase filled with sand. next
time I had the nightmare, when he forced the meat into
my mouth, I bit off the doctor man's index finger at the
knuckle joint and spit it right into his face. woke up,
horrified. never had the nightmare again.

in the second recurring nightmare I was older, maybe nine or ten. I was alone in a big darkened room. there were horizontal windows, long and narrow, but way up high on one wall much taller than all the rest. they had something on them that kept most of the light out. except for a mattress on the floor and a bucket in one corner, the room was empty. this nightmare was not always the same. the room never changed, but there were times when there was no light whatsoever. loud music. too loud to sleep. sometimes there was too much light. a man's voice in the room, probing, calling, yelling. then the same doctor man as the other nightmare. musical voice sometimes soothing soothing. offered me water. food. sometimes the room was too hot. sometimes, too cold. the whole time I was naked, my little girl body

stiff and grey like the inside of a shell, marbled like a skinned pig. but the ending was always the same. me. dead. I felt the deadness deep. no warmth. no life. no home. no me. then I woke up.

I'd heard that beckett was a prolific writer but one other play was especially famous. same period as my childhood. 1950s. endgame. a play with one act, the setting a shelter with four characters. one wheelchair bound and blind. his servant, who couldn't sit. his legless parents, who lived in garbage cans. the shelter was bare except for two small windows high up on a back wall. the right window looked out over the earth, the left out over the sea. the rest of the world was dead. after I read the play, again the ending of the nightmare changed. my daughter––nine or ten at the time–– together with a bear, broke through a wall and helped me get outside. never had the nightmare again.

and there were more beckett connections. beckett was irish, like my dad. had the same birthday. he wrote these two plays in french then translated them into english himself. at the end of grad school I had to write a three hour french language exam. I hadn't taken french since high school, twenty years earlier. I was nervous. rusty. without knowing the topic, I had to read a long literary essay written in french and answer ten questions, in english. the paper I had to read was about french theatre of the absurd, and in particular the two very plays by beckett that transformed my future. the exam was pass fail. I got a strong pass.

The house of sage

bear taught us how to transplant medicines through our dna.

–jimmy o'chiese

every time I gather sage medicine, I smell my late sister. I hear her, giggling, singing, dancing. I feel her relaxed against my back, like when we were girls being quiet on the dry ground in the heat, our eyes looking far away. weaving stories about what we could see, our vision doubled by the pictures in our words. more than twenty-five summers I've gathered sage. horse sage. buffalo sage. bush sage. some I keep, most I pass along to elders, to others who are in need. my late sister and me, twins once again in our giving. that's what we called ourselves. the twins. born less than a year apart, we would joke we shared the same placenta, part of mine saved for hers to grow. often as a child, my twin would dream there was a bear in our room. would sit up frightened and shaking. I would hold her and rock her, tell her how that bear was there to keep us safe. bear was our friend. that's when I first smelled sage.

some years before my twin passed, an elderly couple asked if I would gather sage for them. they were going way down east for ceremony and they wanted to bring a rare and valued gift. I picked for days. my twin was allergic, but even so she helped me dry that sage. filled a duffel bag. on their return the old people called me. said they had something to tell me. a story to share, they said, because my twin and I were there, inside that sage. that's how we often felt my twin and I, inside each other's hearts, our hands touching. pulling at the miles between us, defying space and time. we would read about these things in books with wonder.

as soon as the elderly couple arrived way down east, they were asked to go to a family's home. their teenage son was missing. he was suicidal and he had his dad's shotgun. this was the fourth day. they were frantic. frightened. couldn't breathe. the old couple helped them. asked a relative to fill the house with family and friends, everyone they could find. people came. sat side by side, their backs against every wall of the house, sometimes two and three people deep, a circle of strength and prayer the old people said. then each person took some sage leaves, rolled them into a small ball. they were asked to rub that ball all over their bodies. their heads, their ears and eyes. noses and mouths and throats. arms and legs and bellies and backs and hearts. to put all their pain into that medicine, all their sadness and anger and grief and troubles. clean themselves. sage is a woman's medicine, closest to the heart, the old couple said. just to walk among the sage brings awe and healing, quiet and joy. sage leaves in your shoes, in your pocket, will walk goodness into every move of your day. protect you. after everyone had cleansed themselves, the old couple went all around the house with a plastic grocery bag. asked the people to put the sage into the bag.

my twin died suddenly in her forties. pulmonary embolism. twenty-five years earlier she was sterilized while giving birth to her only child. eugenics society of canada, established in 1930, still going strong. deemed her doubly undesirable: a métis girl with possible depression. they weren't taking any chances, her birthright ripped from her body like trash. no one told her. it was a while before she knew. years.

her world shattered that day. her innocence, her belief in good shook around like a dog at a squirrel. she became depressed, for real. a vivacious young mama, medicated numb. hospitalized, again and again and again. labelled like a lab rat. straightjacketed and shipped to a mental hospital for two and a half years, no visitors allowed. beaten. starved. dragged by her hair. electroconvulsed. the power of a flood light. there was a hole in her memory the size of a house. so many times she just wanted to die, she said, an urge that left her only after that sage medicine made its way to that family way down east. at first she didn't notice, but after she heard the rest of the story, she knew.

after the people gathered in the house put the sage in the bag, the old couple asked them to pray for the boy who was gone, for his safe return home. to pray together as one, as though he was their own son, their own grandson, their own brother, as though these parents' pain and anguish was theirs. and they did. for several minutes, every person prayed. and just as a silence began to fall over the house, the phone rang. it was the tribal police, to say the boy had just arrived, carrying his dad's gun. he was fine, felt good. he was ready to go home. the people in the house had all gathered around, filling the room with a quiet hum, their words like a long and uplifting song the old couple said. they saw that grocery bag in the old man's hand was all lit up, big and bright as a halogen truck light in the middle of the night.

A house full of birds

my story changes all the time. this morning I was asked
to tell stories to little kids. kindergarten to grade six.
the same story. but the story was different with each
grade. a day with children, passing from one story to
the next. so many squeals of laughter. so many little
hands in the air. the older eyes looking down at the
desks until someone farts.

later today a white lady walked up to me at the gym. I
had to take the buds of my ipod out of my ears in order
to hear her. she was not a young woman. she told me
I have very beautiful hair. your long, white hair, she
said. I saw you the other day in red and I knew you
were a beautiful woman who is very spiritual. I know
this because I am a psychologist. I wanted to tell you
that today, she said.

there was another story there, where a girl opened her
mouth and inside was the universe. I saw her there,
overtop lake superior in the dark.

I wish I could be that brave. as brave as the big dipper.
the great bear there, purring, watching, holding my
hand. me looking to the side and down. the words I
seek are buried there, under grief. inside the darkness
of a cottonwood, inside the seeds of orange berries. the
wings of a female mallard in flight, exposing blues and
whites and blacks otherwise unseen, like a woman's
beauty, often hidden until she looks up, sees the small

spaces between the leaves, yellow hearts on the black bark after a fall rain.

something wants to push its way out, from my belly to my heart to the frame of me. a doorframe. a wooden door with windows, an old key that no longer fits. the door to the outside becomes the door to my room, where birds make their way in the early morning light and the wind finds a path through the cracks.

I'm looking, searching my heart for the words, the true words that are buried inside my unruly inner bark. my wood is hard. not hard like something unfriendly, but hard to the seekers of what may be hidden inside, the medicine there.

my hands on my daughter's back, on my grandchildren's feet, my son's shoulders. my heart aches for my own hands. my hands ache to write, to rewrite the torture they endured during childhood. my little girl hands placed in a vice and squeezed, squeezed, squeezed until they were as flat as the coyote after chasing the roadrunner on a desert road. then their release. a pain that defies language. denies anything but silence. half way into terror, half way into another time. they said what is going to happen, happened before, and before that, and will happen again in the future. I believed them. I had to.

my feet, too. placed in a vice. my feet flat like a paper foot. a drawing for a moccasin. so much pain.

 pain waning pain. we are not set up for such things, us people. makes us brave.

I wish I could be that brave. reaching out from the middle of a storm and pulling up people from their flooded homes. opening doors during a flash fire to save a baby. running into the street to pull a child out of the way of a passing bus.

The roadhouse

I've met three people whose loved ones were decapitated by old-growth cedar flying off the back of a flatbed. enjoying the mountain view. I can see an indelible, haunting image every time, the way fresh clearcut's exposed living wood inside the bark creates a pinkish yellow glow. so many tears, longing for the loved ones who used to be. do the forests standing long for their ancestors? do they feel the pain of slaughter? these forests whose grief still seeps the land, the city blocks, the farmers' crops, their stock.

 I was driving through the nighttime mountains, the middle of roger's pass, three others in the car. inside the kind of storm where the snowflakes flood the face with a pinkish bluey glow, the reflection off the headlights on the snow. fernlike stellar dendrites that snow is called. they look like trees. I could see two pins of light growing just ahead on the road. an elk. looked in the rearview. a logging flatbed truck. put the car in neutral, pumped the brake, prayed for the elk on the road, the driver behind us, us. sing-songed hey, hey, hey, hey. hey, hey, hey, hey, over and over again. woke up the ladies in the back seat. saw their eyes reflected in the eyes of the elk on the snow. then the elk disappeared. poof. gone right there off the road.

there used to be millions of elk. not any more, though. now they're endangered. too many clearcuts. migration pathways cut off by highways and roadhouses, farms and fences and towns. pulp mills and refineries and coal mines and trains. so many of the elk who are left have cwd. mad-cow, but the rocky mountain elk kind. giving their brains, their spines a pinkish spongy glow. eating at them from the inside out.

one of my uncles died when he stood up to go pee on a greyhound bus as a moose walked onto the road. just outside wawa. moose are endangered too. global warming. liver and brain parasites. overcrowding. clearcuts. encroachment. the summer before, somewhere south of ottawa, a mature snapping turtle meandered across the highway ahead of my car. plod. plod. plod. plod. I pulled over, stopped both lanes of traffic. picked up that heavy turtle from the middle of the road and took her to a path leading to a lake nearby. snapping turtles are at risk for extinction. egg failure and deformed babies. pinkish spotty shells. pcb's, dioxins, furans, motor oil. squeezed out of their homes. clearcuts. overcrowding. hundreds of calculated road kills every year. for sport. turtles are more than 250,000,000 years old. that's two-hundred-fifty-million. they have come face to face with countless mass extinctions, including the dinosaurs. what does turtle see in the human face?

I once had a neighbour named janice. janice's husband was a violent man. in jail for the brutal beating and sexual assault of their three-year-old baby girl. janice's family was white upper middle class. let janice barely make ends meet. two little kids. took her two years to save up for a car, an old beater that was a rolls to her. it was after dark when she bought that car and insurance companies were closed. wanted to look at it out the picture window of her home so she parked it out on the street. some time in the night, someone hit and totalled her car. fled. a year after that she bought another car.

parked it in a stall out back. that first night someone stole her car. two weeks later she found out her car was totalled in another town. janice asked me, what did I think this might mean?

I told her I think it means sometimes we come face to face with our own human face. if it was me, I'd thank whoever's watching over me and I'd never drive again. janice married another man, a kind and gentle man, had a baby boy. and janice drove again. came by to show me her new station wagon before a road trip through those northern ontario highways with that pinkish rocky glow. her three kids. her. heading for a roadhouse on the side of the road. hit head-on by a logging flatbed truck.

The mad house 1

indigenous natural law: never give up.

–jimmy o'chiese

drove through an early morning sundog. I was heading up sarcee hill, reaching for my sunglasses, the sun just peeking over the crest. ahead on that foothill I could see the western rainbow of the sundog at the ground of the road. moments later, I drove right on through, carried those colours home with me. in

my lunch, in my laundry, in my head. out the big north-facing window at the foot of my bed. that night I couldn't sleep. watched the big pipe rise high to the east and travel its great arch towards the western horizon out the big window of my room.

just after lunch I'd had a call. when I picked up the phone the voice at the other end spoke something into my sundogged ear I couldn't make sense of. said she was the assistant to the dean of grad studies and would I be available for a meeting tuesday with the deans from grad studies and humanities, the head of the english department? my heart pounding in my chest, I quietly asked if she could hold on a moment. put the phone down on a table. waited till my heart stopped its frantic flutter. picked up the phone again. said, sorry about that, to the booming voice of the dean himself.

my thesis was a memoir, a trauma narrative, already approved by the ethics committee. but the men in that tuesday meeting who'd had an earlier discussion among themselves thought it best to have my thesis vetted by the university lawyers before I could defend. that would take about a year. my supervisors were stunned into silence, but helped along by sundog and naivete and an unwavering faith in the power of words, I was strong. words kept me alive, exposed the roots of post traumatic flashback. when I wrote, I knew I was part-way into my spirit-self, holding onto the english language like a gift folded outward, unrestrained by prejudice or fear, forming pictures in the air.

I was reminded of a couple who lived next door to my parents during my late teens. their oldest daughter passed away from cancer at sixteen, after years of holding on. she died at home. spent almost all her time there during her illness. her sisters and brothers spent four of their childhood years with photos of their dying sister all over the walls, and then pictures of her emaciated body in her coffin for years after her death. it'd been twenty years, yet I could look inward and see those photographs with exact clarity.

the tuesday men could give no clear reason for their decision. a few weeks earlier my department head had put a memo in my mailbox. I should pack up my things. my days there were done. I took the memo

to grad studies. met with the women's rep there, a man, who assured me that as long as I was passing, attending classes, doing my work, my department couldn't expel me like in high school. I'd already been

ordered by the dean of humanities to cease all political
work on campus or he'd personally have me up on
misconduct charges. even had to sign a memo. I was
the spokesperson on a small committee of students
elected to act as liaisons between grad students and
faculty. just before I was involuntarily dismissed, we'd
asked that a prof who'd received countless teaching
awards be forced to resign. he was a well-known
resident rapist. violent. used a gun. young, brilliant,
vulnerable women. girls really. everyone knew it. we'd
asked that the department begin to recruit and accept
indigenous students and students of colour into their
grad program. we'd asked too much.

the dean's words left me close and quiet that day,
like back in my mid-twenties. from the office where I
worked then I could hear machines and hammering
and the intimate feel of smoked hide entering my
soft pores. I've always been drawn to the smell of
smoked hide. one morning through their open door,
half-hidden among buckskin gloves and boots and
coats sat two elderly people, a woman and a man. they
motioned to the only other chair, a stool a little higher
than theirs. said I looked like a very beautiful woman
who'd been through a lot of suffering and sacrifice in
my life and they could tell I was a survivor of torture,
like they were. took off their aprons. touched the
tattoos on their arms. said they were happy to have
each other. they were children at auschwitz and
they considered their two adult children their most
successful accomplishment. they said the same thing
as my grandmother. go back to school, they said. go
back to school. be a witness. tell your story.

at thirty-nine, I considered being in a masters
program a great achievement. but my supervisor was
not happy with the direction of my thesis. I told her

I was writing something else I would like to submit,
a memoir, and she agreed to read it. I wanted to write
in a way that refused a voyeuristic reading. I wanted
the reader to truly enter the text, to identify with the
child there, but to be protected from the onslaught of
violence and inexpressible pain. have relief from the
heaviness of the material and yet be

unable to escape, in the same way I was unable
to escape. my past trauma returned in fragments,
interrupted with flashbacks, with my children,
with work, with night terrors, with papers, with
flashbacks, with writing, with personal resistance to
my own past, with night terrors. when she finished
reading the text, she fired me on the spot.

in my youth I'd been fired from a job, but this was
something I didn't see coming, didn't know could
happen. like the elderly couple who encouraged me
to return to school, my supervisor had been kind
and warm. the couple's warmth and kindness was
something I could still feel when I pulled up their
image, their bodies small and inward, their thin faces
looking slightly upward at me. they seemed surreal
and unreal and I felt like vapour, like the smell left
behind inside a hide. their portraits had always stayed
with me, their words motivated me. the smell of hide
returned in that instant. I actually felt them touch me,
felt their eyes inside my own.

my supervisor told me the issue was power. asked,
why did I insist on shoving this stuff down people's
throats? did I write my memoir in my sleep? in
academia, she said, your success was not measured
by how well you write. quoted something from
the bloody monday protests in paris in 1968. said,
we must march through the institutions. I had
no referent. I didn't understand. she seemed to

be encouraging me to protest while telling me to conform. I was too emotional in my writing and that doesn't mean a thing in academia, she continued. said the purpose of grad school was to remind people they are nobodies. I couldn't use anything I'd written and if I wanted this degree I'd have to acquiesce. give it up, she said. give it up. you are shooting yourself in the foot. we are all family here. you are mad, sharron, she said. you are mad.

The mad house 2

I live in chinook country, where trees and trucks and barns and houses get blown around like bits of old paper, fly across fields and highways and towns. I learned about chinooks in grade school. minus forty

to plus twenty in half an hour is what my teacher said. drew a picture of the wind on the board. I created a story from that wind. took what I knew, the ancient sand dunes of the ottawa and a girl who walked through blinding sand storms, eyes down. all the girl could see was her old aunty's feet in front of her at the ground. her aunty would say, we are almost there. watch my feet my girl. never give up. no matter where the two began, that was the story's end. all around the aunty and the girl, beyond the sandy swirl, a childhood scene with sun and rainbows, forest and river and chinook arch and blue. didn't believe any of it.

at nineteen I had to drop out of university after the birth of my son. I was told there were no student loans for single moms in ontario. alberta offered them, though, and I chose to move to calgary. I needed to know the truth of my grade school teacher's stories of warm winds that could push winter far to the east for hours or weeks or days. if I could believe that, then maybe I could believe my own childhood pictures and words all neatly drawn and gridded and hidden inside dust devils on clean white paper, like cartoons in a comic book. I learned a cartoon can be a stand-alone drawing on strong, large paper. so I changed up the form. a cartoon. life size. bright crayon scribbles painted over with black india ink. but willow stick scratches on the surface revealed a new story underneath. clear, living sundog colour blink-blinking out and into the room.

I wrote a new story that way. already I believed in the power of writing. already I knew how words could pull you in, their power unyielding. binding. much like the words that formed my masters thesis. I did find a supervisor who would take me on––two, in fact, as recommended by grad studies. the work was completed and approved when the tuesday men called that first meeting. then, almost a year later to the day, they set up a second gathering. I was offered three what-they-called choices: quit. begin again. defend the trauma narrative––on condition my thesis would be sealed. the university would not publish. my memoir and my research would not appear in the university library, in my supervisors' offices, at the national archives. they took all the original copies the day of my defense, so details of

my theoretical process in the critical afterword were lost to me. I was left with this image of my thesis locked up with tired, haunted, empty eyes, blink-blinking, blink-blinking from inside a darkened vault. much like the eyes of a woman I met in the book store at the children's hospital after my son fractured his skull in his early teens. the woman walked up to me, took my hands into hers and started talking, a young daughter standing in her shadow the whole time. I noticed the girl seemed uncommonly quiet, reserved, like vapour or liquid, while her mother spoke to me. the girl's face remained in my mind's eye, forever there, like a pencil drawing whose lines found their way into the distance around her. the girl's sister had died of cancer a few moments earlier and she was the last of four children, all of whom died of the same cancer. she was the only one cancer-free, the only one to live past ten. the girl's mother said she was bone weary, tired of being spoken to in hushed, quiet tones. I knew that weariness now, what it was like to be handled with kid gloves, when my thesis was sealed. then again when the trauma narrative section of my thesis was published by press gang publishers. to the editors (even though there was virtually no editing done) I was not a writer at all, but an adult victim of unfathomable childhood atrocities. again lawyers were involved. I had to write under a pseudonym, beckylane. I felt like the little girl in the hospital, eclipsed by her siblings' deaths, the little girl in my childhood stories, obscured by whirling sand. flat and invisible.

I needed to write my trauma narrative in order to develop a writing career, albeit undermined. in more ways than I care to say I've been kept out of the local writers' loop. all be that understated. a few years after I graduated, the late rita joe, mi'kmaw elder and writer—— who received the order of canada——read my memoir in the night. let her bacon and eggs get cold the next morning. said, when a child is asked to make that kind of sacrifice she's rewarded ten-fold during her adult years. I've met the queen, she said. I asked after her grandkids. you're not supposed to make the queen laugh, she said. not supposed to talk to her. then rita joe told me, keep doing the work you do, my girl. keep writing. keep questioning and keep pushing at authority. otherwise us indians will get nowhere. rita joe's words that day——

the ones I can share and the ones I cannot--helped me
to understand what happened when I presented my
thesis to the english department and graduate studies at
the university of calgary in a new

and deeper way. unpublished theses are rare,
particularly when they have already been vetted
and approved by the university ethics committee. a
reminder of the power of fear. the power of words.
never give up, rita joe said. never give up.

The mad house 3

to a cynic or a skeptic, what I'm about to recount may
seem way out there. for us métis, the figure eight
embodies infinity, the indestructibility of our nation.
two cultures that cannot be torn apart. forever. a
couple summers ago I was at a ceremony. the people
there were invited to hang the flag of their nation.
flagpoles all dressed and lined up, one after the other
after the other, four days and nights. nation after
nation. the métis flag flapped a strong-wind-flap the
whole time. blue and white, blue and white, horizontal
in the wind every moment. like the current of a river,
a continuous, steady flow. what's important to know
is there were hours at a time when the air was still
and hot and dry and all the other flags drooped and
sagged, slack. hugging the poles. there was a great
deal of speculation. lots of talk. there were questions
and there was fear. and there was great joy and pride
among us métis. the babies and the kids, the teens.
the ladies and the men and the old people. even after
all the suppression, the silencing, the shaming we
endured over the past five hundred years, we knew our
ancestors were there. we knew we were protected. we
knew we were doing the right thing.

sometimes life is simple like that. even when fear inserts itself, a miracle breaks apart a long-sleeping silence. there is so much more to know. in my own writing life, how could I have known the silencing I would endure when my thesis was censored by the university? when I had no choice but to publish my trauma narrative under a pseudonym? how could I have known how much both of these events would undermine my literary career? cause untold damage and harm? dishonour and shame? I felt silenced for years.

after two years my memoir was out of print. then about ten years ago tlicho writer richard van camp listed where the rivers join among the top ten books by indigenous writers in english. held up a copy when I was reading at a west coast line launch. declared, this book saves lives! someone said it was still among the most signed-out books at regina public library. some interest was stirred up to republish. I received calls from four publishers. asked to provide a reading copy at three more. every one declined. a typical response, and I quote: we did have a chance to review your memoir, previously published by

press gang, and unfortunately don't feel this is something that we can include in our reprint program at this time. and, we were concerned about including a title on ritual abuse, because as a cultural phenomenon it has been largely discredited as a moral panic of the 1980s and 1990s. and, for this book, you might consider having it published electronically through amazon, so that you can ensure its viability as a source for anyone who might like to research the topic of ritual abuse. and, I do note that we found your prose both strong and very readable.

then at an international auto/biography conference
in banff this past spring, there was a woman who spit
her food onto her plate. she heard me read the previous
day and I was good, she said. like most of the scholars
there she'd never heard of me and was wondering why.
tell me the titles of your books from the most recent to
the first. I said, some of the titles are long. no problem,
she said, her attention divided between me and her
chicken parmesan. I listed the titles slowly. watched
her body begin to fold in on itself in disinterest, her
eyes dart from chair to chair searching for a break
in a conversation. when I got to the title of my first
book, I felt like I was in a movie set. her food flew from
her mouth in a perfect triangular spray like a monty
python moment. the colour drained from her face. she
white knuckled the edge of the table and pushed back
her chair to get a better look into my face. her voice
shrill and loud, she almost hollered, you are beckylane?
I told her, no.

I am not beckylane. beckylane does not exist, just
as my masters thesis doesn't exist, sealed as it is
inside a vault. my masters degree was not classified
as a creative writing degree but as a research english
degree in feminist bio-theory. that's what it says on
my certificate, something that neither describes my
work nor my scholarly interests. in her foreword, lee
maracle concluded with, I am moved to wonder at the
amazing things this spirited and heroic woman could
have accomplished had she not been forced upon this
path. lee maracle had no idea that when I finally did
tell my story, I was forced to walk backwards into the
oncoming traffic of that same path. to deny my very
existence. I was bullied there. yet it could be argued
that I wasn't forced into this long-sleeping silence. that
is true. this long-sleeping silence was forced into me.
such is the power of silencing through shaming.

silencing through shaming. last winter I was away at a nephew's wedding. my dad passed away while I was there. I wasn't rushing home. when asked why, I shared some from my early life. the cousins opened up about their years in residential school. in métis boarding school. torture. starvation. sexual assault. no contact with brothers for sisters, sisters for brothers. forbidden to speak the language. no parents. no grandparents. no family whatsoever. no culture. no ceremony. no traditions. inferiority bashed and beaten into their tiny bodies. their minds. their hearts. their spirits. over and over again. canada's official policy: genocide. kill the indian within the child.

my cousins' aging faces, locked and frozen in my mind. not vapour or pencil or photographs on a wall but skin and heart and bone. years of flashbacks. trauma. depression. suicide. to stay alive is the challenge. at age seven I attempted suicide. I'd been hurt so bad I couldn't talk. completely lost my voice. weeks later I found my way to the porch of our house, stood on a stool. stared at myself in a mirror. I hated me. I wanted to die. I smashed the mirror with my fists, sliced my little arms, my legs, my chest. that was the moment my voice returned.

The queer house 1

to my mom, lesbians were a whole other kind of species, and I grew to look at them like aliens. if not for the term two-spirit, I probably wouldn't have self identified, and had the opportunity to talk about gay relationships as natural, and not something we have been socialized to see as not normal.

–amanda ribbonleg-mills, two-spirit youth

homophobia and transphobia are like greedy giants hiding behind a wall of fear––calling, yelling, screaming. hate. fear. hate. fear before the face of knowledge can be a dangerous, evil creature. part of my life's work is to dispel some of the fear that festers inside homophobia. inside transphobia. inside racism and sexism and the fear of poverty that keeps capitalism aching like a maggot-infested limb. for years I was trapped inside my own beautiful lesbian, homophobic self. I had no idea what to do. where to turn. in my family, with my friends, my community.

childhood was when I knew my heart was for women. I was fortunate. my métis grandmère loved a woman. closeted most of her adult life. she gave me one of those giant webster's for my fourth birthday. I thought that dictionary was a story book. every time she'd visit, she'd sit there on my mom's phone chair, open that book, point to a word, and tell a story long as your arm. words have supernatural powers, she'd say. words are sacred, so be careful what you say, ma petite. be careful what you call yourself.

when I was sixteen my grandmère showed me the word lesbian. she burst out laughing at that word, all capitalized and important. look at this, my girl. lesbian is: 1. a native or inhabitant of lesbos, an island of greece, off turkey, 623 square miles; or, 2. of, pertaining to, or characteristic of sappho or her poetry. I wondered why the sound of lesbian was so funny to her and why she pointed out this word to me so often. years later I realized she must have sensed something in me I didn't yet acknowledge in myself.

true, all my crushes were on other girls and women from my first crush on, but I thought there was something wrong with me. and I certainly didn't refer to myself as a lesbian. I mean, what did an island off turkey have to do with me? and I would be the first to admit that I loved poetry, but who the heck was sappho?

when my daughter is sixteen she wants to know if we can give back to the community by taking in foster kids. siblings, two little ones. you're a good mom, mom. I've always wanted little brothers or sisters. so, together we take the training with métis foster parenting services. we are excited. then in our final interview I'm asked to leave my girl in the waiting area. I sit with three women. none of them meets my eyes. one is the manager. she tells me I am not a good fit for fostering children. I seem to be an awesome mom and my knowledge and experience with children is extensive. but you are a lesbian. the whole time she is talking down at her outstretched hands. we cannot have a lesbian mothering our children. you understand. we just can't have it. you might turn the children to go that way.

years before I came out to my family and friends as a lesbian, I would crouch down between rows of tall books at the university library reading anthropological and missionary accounts of women's two- spirit stories. I felt like a criminal sitting on that dusty floor reading about myself in books that were published at the turn of the 20th century. by then I'd learned the word berdache. for a while I tried to move my mouth around that word and make it me, but I was afraid. I was catholic and I was a good girl. my mom despised lesbians. filled her with terror and dread and loathing. I was married to a man but I continued to like women. and besides, that word for indian homosexual wasn't even in my grandmère's dictionary. so I printed berdache all neat on a nice piece of paper and pasted it right there between bereave and berchtesgaden.

in my early thirties––about the same time I presented myself as a woman who loves women, I learned the history of the word berdache. the root was introduced into european languages through muslim contact, and by the time they came to our shores, the french were using berdache to mean catamite, a younger man or boy who was used as a sex slave. in europe, berdache referred to male homosexuals in general, but by the mid-1800s the word wasn't used at all. except in north america. manipulated by missionaries and anthropologists to describe what they perceived to be homosexual indigenous peoples. there were and are already words in the first languages to describe people who did not live and love as heterosexuals from a european worldview. these people were not sexualized. anthropologists and missionaries would have known this.

I'm visiting some friends way up north, at a métis settlement. we have a great time throughout the couple weeks I'm there. the plan is we'll go to edmonton together, stay in a hotel for a few days, then I'll hop a bus home. several hours into our trip we stop to eat at a lone restaurant. there doesn't even seem to be a town around. it's raining heavily. after lunch I go and use the washroom. I walk outside to an empty parking lot, my bags soaking in the rain. we were to meet a girl in her late teens in edmonton. she would be testifying in court and they were going there to support her. she was one of dozens of métis and native youth they've fostered over the years. I find a wet note tucked into my bags. the problem? she would have to sleep in the same bed as me in the hotel. they were afraid I would sexually assault her.

fully adult with kids of my own and I still didn't have that word. then, in winnipeg in 1990, at the third annual gathering of indigenous lesbian, gay, bisexual and transgendered peoples, participants embraced the term two-spirit, the english translation of the anishinaubae, niizh manitoag. I respect that there are many who do not identify with what has now become pan-indigenous, but this one caused me to remember my grandmère's promise. words are sacred, she said. be careful what you call yourself. for me, this one finally fit.

The queer house 2

two-spirits are busy in the effort to decolonize and help out each other and all their relatives, which I think is what warriors really do in this day and age. now, that sort of role, I like that very much, it suits me, and it doesn't rest on the assumption that there must be some sort of counterproductive gender or sex based hostility.

–carla osborne, two-spirit youth

I'm asked to speak about two-spirit people in an english course at a university in calgary. they have read one of my books, she walks for days/ inside a thousand eyes/ a two-spirit story. the native students in the class approach me afterwards to see if I'll speak about two-spirit people during one of their brown bag lunches at the native centre. I tell them, sure. so they go ahead and put a notice on their events board. a few days before the proposed talk I get a call from the director. wants to meet with me. fidgets with the seam of a shirt sleeve throughout our meeting, pulling at a loose thread. hands visibly shaky. informs me there is no issue with homophobia in the native centre. a talk of this kind will only stir up problems that are not there. not interested in my input. stands up and motions to the door, still no eye contact, face flushed. you are not welcome to do a talk on lesbians or gays or queers or trannies or two-spirits or whatever you call yourselves. ever.

when I was still in grade school, my friend's granny told us a story. before contact, white men had been trained to kill their women, she said. boys went to boarding schools. they had no mothers. for a few hundred years they'd been turning in their own auntys and sisters, mothers and friends, grandmothers

and wives and cousins, to be quartered or beheaded or burned alive as witches. you can imagine their fright when they saw our other genders, those who weren't heterosexual in the white man's narrow gender view? very fancy, they were, she said. very visible. there were many what granny called other genders, who dressed and lived and danced and prayed different in ceremony. it didn't take long for the white man to notice this, and they started a mass slaughter of the other genders. thought they were evil. witches. the elders then taught those remaining to blend in, in order to preserve the ancient knowledge held by them. many were medicine people, healers and midwives. child care workers. mediators and warriors. singers.

granny went on to say that the way she learned it from her grandmother, we're all made up of two sides, two spirits––the female and the male. the left side, the side closest to the heart, is the female side. the right is male. when a woman and man marry, the male in the man balances with the male in the woman and the female in the woman balances with the female in the man and they become like one spirit that way. but with the other genders, they have that balance of male and female already, being complete in that way. so, you see, my girls, she said, they can be with a man, a woman or on their own because of that balance.

a couple years ago this medicine man I know asks me to help out sometimes. tells me he works with two-spirit youth in the schools. in the system and in ceremony.

could use my advice. my first-hand experience. invites me to come help at a ceremony where there'll be young two-spirit women. in the early hours of the morning that first night he says he wants to talk to all the women. his eyes dart back and forth on the ground. talks that way, his words welted and swollen with a mix of anger and fright. says women have no place at ceremony. that there's a reason women were excluded from ceremony long time ago. nothing but a bunch of gossips. a bunch of complainers. don't want to hear a word from any of you. his face changes then. reddens. almost looks up. he wants all the lesbians to come tell him they are lesbian. they will have to sleep separate from the other women. not fair for the normal women to have to change in front of your types.

over the years, I've been in situations where homophobic folks have thrown rocks at me, pushed me down stairs, spit in my face. where homophobic students have literally turned their backs to me like in a choreographed dance. to help somehow make good change I offer to lead a series of homophobia workshops for native people and people of colour at a university. the turnout is incredible. during the introduction circle one of the women stands. she is shaking, her fists clenched. she raises her voice to a scream. she spits on those around her. overpowers the small room. insists she speaks for everyone there. you are a sick lady. a horrible, evil, vile thing. a monster. a snake. a spawn of the devil. you need help. if I would have known this workshop was about, about, you people, I would never have come. would never have brought my kids to this poison place, that's for sure. when she finally sits, exhausted, I ask her if she would like to take a break. she shakes her head yes. we haven't completed the circle yet so I ask the others if they're okay with that. they shake their heads yes. I suggest we take a fifteen minute break. I tell them, we're here every saturday for the next six weeks. anyone who feels they can't stay? that's okay.

the woman? she returns. becomes a strong ally. they all do. I continued to lead workshops with a goal to empowerment and healing of indigenous two-spirit peoples and their allies. focused on life's day-to- day. returning to the land. cultural reclamation, transforming negative myths. healing broken families who suffer from homophobia and transphobia. two-spirit peoples are grandparents and parents, daughters and sons, cousins, auntys, uncles. friends. talked about our histories and cultures. our own identities and families. watched films and tracked reactions. came up with positive ways to make change. shared knowledge. discussed why two-spirit youth move to towns and cities and how that impacts our communities and well being. two-spirit youth came and spoke.

until I was thirty years old I was trapped inside my own beautiful two-spirit, homophobic self and I had no idea what to do, where to turn. I wrote little notes on bits of paper and napkins just to let out my feelings. the very act of writing at all was an act of activism. in my parents' home, when I was married to a man, I had no privacy so I'd toss out all the notes. the final day I was in the marriage house, I went from room to room to make sure nothing was left behind. as I swept my hand over the upper shelf of one of the closets, I came across piles and piles of notes. my ex had retrieved them from the trash. left them there for me to find. I felt so violated. sat right there on the floor. read through them and wept. wept for myself. for the invasion of my privacy. how trapped I'd felt and how I'd wanted to leave for years. to escape the violence. the verbal abuse. the sexual assaults. the last note I read went like this:

each person I touch, whether by happenstance or by choice, is as much a part of me as I am of myself. we are all related. there is so much mystery. colour inside bone. I am red. I am read. I will leave this man. I will come out. I will give back. I will write my story.

The red paper house

in spite of all government attempts to convince indians to accept the white paper, their efforts will fail, because indians understand that the path outlined by the department of indian affairs through its mouthpiece, the honourable mr. chrétien, leads directly to cultural genocide. we will not walk this path.

–harold cardinal, 1969

it all started on my birthday, the day after pierre trudeau got sworn in. his picture was above the chalk board. teacher stood me up in front of the class. used a wooden stick to point out parts of my body. started at my head. dull-witted blue-eyed indian she said, teacher's lips a thin pink line. can't be trusted. shifty. look at her smile there, it's upside down. now that's a frown. show us all your rotten teeth. poked at my mouth. teacher started that way and worked her way down. lifted at the hem of my orange flowered skirt. she'll never finish school. by fifteen she'll be pregnant like all the other two-bit squaws.

so I focused on my love of drawing. of detail. a schoolmate and I were chosen to fill the hallways with murals. hired in the summer to draw and colour maps. the arts cushioned me, covered me. sang to me, through a coloured pencil, through a paint brush, through a book. I wanted to know how words could dig under the skin like that. bleed through kindness and trust. even before I learned to talk, I felt their power, words. my irish grampa was a traditional storyteller. his stories captivated people. his tone, the way he moved his body, his eyes. his cruelty at home. controlled the people, the world around him. loud belly laughter seeped in deep seated shame.

nineteen and pregnant, I met pierre trudeau, intersection of elgin and sparks. culture shocked and attending carleton university on a scholarship, I'd never yet in my life been in either a restaurant or a mall. I remember him as a lone leprechaun in a pale green suit standing just below me, already on the road. I took a double look, his eyes meeting mine. said he looked just like pierre trudeau. he shifted so I could see his red, red rose. his voice honey velvet like my grampa's, but his smile full-toothed, I am pierre trudeau. I looked down at those teeth and thought of his white paper. how he tried to make the treaties obsolete. abolish the indian act. eliminate status. convert reserve land to private property. wipe canada's slate clean. complete that crime of genocide once and for all. I said as much, gave him a crooked-toothed grin, then turned to walk back the other way.

trudeau used to take walks in the snow to help him think. white washed. me, later that day I walked the maples in full fall red. my thoughts drifted back to '63, when canadian civil rights activists started to ask questions about canada's treatment of first peoples here at home. canada hired an anthropologist. wrote his citizens minus report. advised the feds to end enforced assimilation, residential schools. provide resources, opportunities, choices. the feds distributed

a pamphlet, choosing a path, organized first peoples'
meetings, brought band members to ottawa. first
peoples' recommendations? turn to natural law. begin a
process of reconnection for the true owners of the land,
those not yet born. uphold first peoples' and treaty
rights, land title, self-determination. provide access to
education. health care.

 ottawa's answer by '69? the white paper. first peoples'
response? put that natural law in writing the following
year. citizens plus, the red paper.

it's been almost fifty years since I looked down on
trudeau that crisp fall day. the last residential school
closed when he was an old man, in 1996. and now
I'm getting old myself. after the royal commission
on aboriginal peoples report, after the apology from
the prime minister (presented and televised during
working hours on a work day when most canadians
were not in front of their tvs at home). after the truth
and reconciliation interim report? first peoples'
concerns are pretty much the same. still unaddressed.
behind one closed door on parliament hill the trc
stands still. through the closed door across the hall, the
parties pass bill after undermining bill. trudeau is now
long dead. his christmas present baby high school phys
ed teacher son now leads the government. he quotes to
the press, "like someone who was raised by wolves."
pricked by a red, red rose.

A house shared by bees

*we honour our mothers as much as our fathers. why are we
ourselves preoccupied with what amount of mixture we have of
european and indian blood? for if we have some of one and the
other, doesn't acknowledgement and filial love make for us one
law which says: "we are métis."*

–louis riel

here's the thing. heard of the daniels ruling? january
8th, 2013? appealed by the feds less than a month later,
so maybe not. but then it was upheld by the feds in
their court of appeal a couple of aprils later, so maybe.
what the daniels ruling basically means is us métis are
indians again. first time since before the indian act,
when we'd never been anything but. and the feds? they
didn't pass the daniels ruling to promote the métis
nation. they plan to quantum us, make métis extinct.

me, I'm shaped by a métis mother whose family
scattered after the indian act to escape apartheid and
persecution. crossed the river into ottawa, only to see
my mom, her brothers and sisters––all six of them,
scooped by strangers in a big black car. raised with
unspeakable brutality by outsiders in foster homes on
isolated farms in rural ontario.

neonicotinoids? nicotine-derived insecticides. heard of them? a little later the same year. september 13, 2013, health canada confirms neonicotinoids are killing all the bees, the pollinators. 200 million acres are sprayed with this chemical. makes its way into the pollens, the plant life, the soils, the ground water. a hive of bees visits about 225 thousand flowers every day. a single bee up to several thousand. and health canada? they're not going to ban the poison. they're going to make the labels bigger, make bees extinct.

me, I'm allergic to bees. got stung during childhood and almost died. carried an epipen ever since. there've been honey bees living at three of my houses, their nectar lining the walls, their hum like dueling fiddles before sunrise, after dark. last year there were honey bees behind the cedar siding of my brother's house. he climbed a ladder and started spraying their nest. a semi-transparent bee the size of a hummingbird appeared. hovered, looked him straight in the eye. reminding us––without bees, there is no life.

let's look each other straight in the eye, canada. honey bees, like indians, have a round dance inside the privacy of their hive to tell the others there is food nearby. like métis, honey bees have a waggle dance, a jig in the shape of the infinity symbol, to tell the others the direction and distance of food further away. to us métis the infinity symbol represents the immortality of our nation, two cultures that cannot be torn apart.

then in 2014 the feds start telling our newly indianized youth they're 1/16th, the last generation of métis. tell them their kids aren't métis.

the daniels ruling has no meaning for us, canada. we've lived in longhouses, wigwams, tipis, tents, cabins, road allowances, squatting places, logging camps, mining camps, boarding schools, orphanages, sanatoriums, foster homes, adoptive homes, group homes, prisons, half-way houses, settlements, reserves, streets, ditches, shelters, safe houses, crown land, cities, villages, villages within villages, towns within towns. we are everywhere in canada, everywhere in the americas. face it, canada–– without métis, there is no life.

The house of stakes and crosses

december, 2012. bill c-45 breaches canada's own laws on the fiduciary legal duty to consult and accommodate first nations. the canadian government just gave birth to a monster.

–grand chief stan beardy

I have a dream this morning where a yellow and a black swallowtail butterfly are flying, dancing around in the front seat of my car. a kaleidoscope of yellow swallowtails appears in some nearby black poplars. they keep coming and coming and coming, yellow after yellow after yellow. occasionally one swallowtail is black. I didn't know the blacks born to the yellows are female until the black butterfly in my car hovers at my left ear, whispers, listen for what's on the ground, my girl. listen for the water.

the last time I saw a black swallowtail flying together with a yellow was overtop the upper waters of niagara falls, the rock underneath shaped like a butterfly in flight. the wings of that great waterway empty one-fifth of mother earth's fresh water over a falls where white folks like annie edson-taylor hurled herself over the edge inside a coffin-like barrel and maria spelterini tight-roped across the gorge with a paper bag over her head and woven baskets on her feet. as if trying to touch the spirit of the wyendot maid of the mist, who lived for a time behind the falls with the thunderbeings, their voices still heard there today.

at contact, there were thriving wyendot trading centres not far from niagara falls. cities housed about two hundred wooden buildings surrounded by hundreds of miles of trails and dozens of towns. vast stores of food for each city and town. fresh water. sewage and waste disposal. tobacco grown inside the towns and outside, hundreds of acres of corn. eight different squash, sixty beans. sugar maples. thirty-four fruits, eleven nuts. fifty other wild foods. the land passed from mother to daughter, generation after generation, at least 10,000 years.

then a settlers' claim post. one of europe's little miracles. drive a stake or erect a cross on someone else's land and, poof. it's yours. a kind of sorcery. english, french, spanish, portuguese, danish, swedish, norse––the good old white boys' stakes and crosses greatest race.

the old métis had their eyes fixed on a different race. that time long ago when trickster challenged an enormous round stone to a great race. this was way back when the great lakes were all still ice. to begin the race, trickster pushed the round stone to a hilly rolling place. they ran faster and faster down that hill. hundreds of kilometres with stone in the lead. when trickster finally caught up, that mouth ran faster than those legs, mocking and taunting and teasing stone. trickster raced down ahead of stone hundreds of more miles and then fell right there on the path, dead asleep. just like that, drool dribbling from mouth to nose and back again.

when stone finally caught up to the snoring trickster, there was one rude awakening for both of them. with nowhere else to go, stone's roll ended with an abrupt splat, flat on trickster's back. trickster's bony shoulders stopped that stone cold. many years passed that way, with trickster trapped under the weight

of stone, ice melting all around them. then as one long winter transformed to spring, the thunderbeings saw that trickster was close to drowning. close to starving. they sent bolts of lightning. shattered ice and stone and set the two friends free. in milliseconds, millions of swallowtail butterflies, yellows and blacks, came out from in the trees, caught stone's dismembered parts. tenderly laid them down right there on the ground in the shape of a giant butterfly, changing the path of one-fifth of mother earth's flow over stone's newly formed butterfly back––out to the mouth of the eastern sea.

as soon as they were freed the two friends drank from that sacred water there. then trickster could be seen flying west on a soft yellow bed of swallowtails––with the occasional black. set trickster down from time to time for a big feast, helped put some fat on those bones along the way. to express sincerest gratitude, trickster gave the swallowtails new spots on their tails––a splash of red and blue and white–– sent them to live in the four directions of turtle island. then trickster gave them a gift to share with the people. ever since that day it is said if you want a wish to come true, whisper your wish to a swallowtail.

as I was waking up from that early morning butterfly dream, a swallowtail lingered, as if caught between the worlds. whispered. I made a wish––to help remove the monster that's bill c-45 from the backs of the politicians on parliament hill. I asked the thunderbeings to smash that bill into millions of pieces. free the 32,000 larger lakes and the thousands upon thousands of smaller ones. free the 2,250,000 rivers who are in danger of extinction. free all the sacred waters that are staked to that

legalese bill. liberate mother earth's waters out from under the settler's cross.

The house that's idle no more

kids wanna be so bad
but in my dreams we're still screamin
and runnin through the yard

– ❤ , authored by "heart symbol"
(10th street bridge, calgary, 2011)

the slaughter of two million
buffalo a year, five full years
the white man proud
those bones, heaped trophies

– ❤ (10th street bridge, calgary, 2011)

writings on the 10th street bridge. distracting thousands in their rush hour daze. traffic under bridges, over roads. native youth who write on the railing walls, only to be painted over. over and over again. words on top of words, their ink thick with hope. these kids know who they are. they are speaking out, their poems written on bridges, on the screens of their phones, a continuous story of what it is to be an ndn kid in canada today. the waters sacred, flooding downtown and their poems a testament to their patience.

mohawk wisdom––
the heart is the strength of life
of all races
all nations

> **– ♥ (10th street bridge, calgary, 2012)**

these kids know things other kids don't know about
the limits of life. nunavut. daniels decision. indian act.
white paper. buffalo jump report. residential schools.
charlottetown accord. oka crisis. harper's plan. redbook
burning. indian problem. murdered women and girls.
attawapiskat. barriere lake. enbridge northern gateway.
oil sands. pacific trails pipelines. fracking. elsipogtog.
missing women and girls. rexton. flash mobs. round
dances. generations of stories like their own.

idle no more calls on all people
to join in a peaceful revolution
to honour indigenous sovereignty
to protect the land and water

> **– ♥ (placard, 10th street bridge, calgary, 2013)**

idle no more
ban bill c-45

> **– ♥ (10th street bridge, calgary, 2012)**

writings on the 10th street bridge. replaced with poppy
plaza and the three-lane rush. let's get face to face.
there's something in the air, and these kids aren't going
anywhere. the guardian in the uk says, first nation's
peoples––and the decision of canadians to stand
alongside them––will determine the fate of the planet.
it is said that only good comes from struggle. good.

The house filled with buckshot

apparently this is the new way of consultations. government speaks, "you bring the drum, we'll bring the guns."

–duncan mercredi

helen betty osborne, 19. november 13th, 1971. brutally raped and slaughtered by 4 white men. charges brought up 16 years later. aboriginal justice implementation commission sites racism, sexism and indifference by rcmp. because they could.

an old story, their red coats dyed in the blood of indians. why just yesterday harper gives his throne speech. plans to empower the military and focus on the extinction of rivers and resources. so many fancy words. today peaceful people protest fracking on their homeland. met with rcmp snipers hidden in the grass. that's the plan.

connie jacobs, 37, her 9-year old son ty and her unborn child. march 22nd, 1998. shotgunned and killed by rcmp. because she was standing in a doorway.

lance cutarm, 32. august 3rd, 2013. shot and killed by rcmp. because he was walking down the road.

I'll be brief. it all started when they hanged kah paypamahchukways and pah pah-me-kee-sick, manhoose and kit-ahwah-ke-ni and nahpase. a-pis-chas-koos and itka, waywahnitcheight and louis riel in 1885. six were from big bear's band. poundmaker and big bear were sent to jail. all for rising up after smallpox-infested blankets that were given as gifts decimated their people, followed up by forced starvation, the slaughter of millions upon millions of buffalo. then there's kisse-manito wayo twelve years later. refused permission from the local indian agent to kill his own cattle to feed his starving extended family, so killed one anyway. cannoned by a hundred rcmp officers and good white settler men. got their muskets all heated up. but that was then and this is now.

been the plan all along. right there in the shadow of the rcmp, child welfare's fat cash cow. the latest in residential schools. they try to screen foster families, but there's not always time. too many little indian children being grabbed from their homes. why in calgary alone a few dozen families busted up every month. white ladies go in, little native children herded out. but some babies don't make it home. like the rcmp, child welfare's shooting for mass graves. their five-year record stands alone.

lee allan bonneau, 6 years old. august 21st, 2013. beaten to death while in the system.

june alexus dawn goforth, 4 years old. august 2nd, 2012. beaten to death while in the system.

genesis vandell parenteau-dillon, 13 months old. november 1st, 2011. beaten to death while in the system.

evander lee daniels, 22 months old. june 8th, 2010. drowns in scalding water while in the system.

unnamed indian child, 3 years old. december 17th, 2009. left in bed to die while in the system.

the facts are out. in the past 15 years, 145 children have died while in the system in alberta. still it goes on. still mommies of our babies are murdered every day. still young girls and women disappear. at least eleven hundred in the last twenty years. same as forty thousand white ladies. as the u.n. investigates, canada retaliates. there is a story here. but there are no heroes in this story. sir john a said, let's obliterate the indian. they're nothing but a problem. harper says, I'm sorry. send in the troops.

The quilting house

I once heard a story where women sew a quilt from men's eyes. just one quick look, and a young man's eyes fly out from his sockets, leaving him blind and wandering until he dies. his eyes continue to live on, blinking out at the world. then one young man turns into a duck and enters one of the women, who gives birth to a son. when he reaches a certain age, that son kills all the women, including his mother, and returns the eyes to the men's bones, who are then revived to their former selves. I was young at the time and I was told the story was about the fear of women's creativity, women's power, the fear of women working together. I didn't understand. I was disturbed, confused. afraid to associate myself with such blatant, deliberate brutality.

I hadn't thought about the story in many years, until I heard a group of old ladies move deep into song. they all had hand drums. at first they were smiling and looking at one another, and then they all closed their eyes at the same time. it was like they moved to another place and they took the rest of us with them, all of us like bees on bright red flowers, our bodies bent into themselves. I instantly understood-- without doubt or hesitation--how love resides there, inside the heart, between beats. and I finally understood that fear of the power of women's creativity.

my body was still bending long after the women stopped. my name, nothing was the same. I felt like I'd been turned inside out, my bones exposed and left there to save me.

the old ladies gathered us all in a circle to go around and greet one another. I was standing next to one of them. I heard a young woman ask if the old lady considered herself a feminist, and the old lady put her right hand over her mouth, laughing. a warrior woman's song is for all of us, she said. if you sing that song and you feel like a feminist, find your sisters who follow that way. see if it's for you. we all need each other. it is important to support all that we do, whether we agree or disagree. be kind to one another. us older ladies, we're taught to speak only of ourselves when we talk. no gossip that way. helps us learn. listen, my girl. throughout your days use all your senses, even your sight, with your eyes closed.

the old lady turned to her left to hug the woman there and it was then that I saw she was wearing a shawl made with the softest, pale deer hide, hanging straight down her narrow back. the fringe was thinly cut, longer than a woman's arm, hugging the floor. all along the back of her shawl, from her neck to her fringe, were rows and rows of tiny beaded eyes. the eyes were all closed, set deep inside sockets. they looked alive, as though they would pop open and look into mine.

the old lady felt my eyes on her back. she turned, smiled. winked. then continued around the circle.

The straw man's house

*where does the colossal task of decolonization fit into
reconciliation?*

–graham angus

I have a dream with maliseet elder shirley bear, a lady
who preserves and passes knowledge to keep the
traditions alive. orally, in her art work, her writings.
her activist work. her intimate knowledge of women's
roles in matrilineal indigenous societies. she is well
travelled, was involved in a.i.m. bill c-31. received the
order of canada. she works tirelessly for indigenous
women and the seven generations who follow. as she
and many elders say, most of the adults in indigenous
cultures suffer the effects of residential schools. the
indian act. enforced euro-mindset church and nation
state. power and control. brutality. torture. domination
and greed. genocide. one day, though, that will all
change. women will teach the young to re-learn.

shirley bear once said, if you don't help people, what's
the point of living? in my dream, she's driving with
me in my car. I'm excited for her to see the ottawa
river valley, where I grew up. we're on our way to
ceremony, heading southeast where the water is wide
as a lake. when the silver blue comes into view the road
transforms to river and we are in a canoe together. the

shores are lined with deep blood-red willow, first signs of spring. but this is no ordinary river. turns out we're travelling on a guswentah, a two-row wampum. parallel to us a motor boat whizzes by, then cuts us off, white people waving.

how quickly the euro-mindset forgets. the two-row wampum is a nation-state-to-nation-state treaty, not pretty pictures on a beaded belt. a living document, the guswentah is known as the silver covenant chain. embodies the principle of respect. sharing and mutual recognition. partnership. a guswentah honours the jurisdiction of each nation. their mutual authority. autonomy. automatically. forms the foundation for all treaties with colonial europeans. first the dutch in 1645. the british in 1664. two paths. two vessels travel the same river of life. one a birch bark canoe: the original peoples. the laws and customs. the ways. the other a boat: european peoples. their laws and customs and ways. neither tries to steer or overpower the other. the nations' promise is to come together regularly to polish the chain, to feast and talk, to restore the original friendship. to pass the treaty down from generation to generation so that its intent is never forgotten.

deep blood-red willow along the shoreline in my dream. red willow. a potent, powerful medicine in the hands of someone working for the good of the people. in danger, a person with a red willow stick can

grow longer legs for getaway. transform a log to a monster, a dog to a bear. make food appear. and when crafted and aimed in a good and prayerful way, a red willow arrow will never miss its mark.

there is a haudenosaunee two-headed serpent prophecy, told to the five nations of the iroquois confederacy long before the guswentah of 1664, long before the arrival of europeans in their boats. it is said the two heads of the giant are post-contact euro-church and euro-state. we have reached the years of the prophecy where one head will begin to eat the other. same time, the remaining head will begin to destroy itself from the inside out. all those who've been enslaved by that living head will rise up against it. distracted, that remaining head will not notice a young boy. the young boy will make a bow with the hair of the clanmothers. arrows from red willow. those arrows' true aim will fly deep into the heads of the two-headed serpent. the boy will climb the huge belly of the carcass, slice it open, and all the real people eaten by the two-headed monster will be liberated. there will then be a rich vitality not seen since the coming of the two-headed serpent. now is that time. the women are teaching the young to re- learn.

Art house

flowers came as gifts from the star children. before that
time, spring didn't bring crocuses to the south facing
hills or delicate flowers throughout the meadows.
shooting stars, bluebells, buffalo beans, violets, ladies
moccasins, cherry blossoms, apple blooms, roses,
lilacs, starbursts. no sweetness in the air. no harvests
of fruits or berries or vegetables transformed from
their flowery beginnings.

métis are called the flower beadwork people. the
art of beadworking has thrived among indigenous
women and men for centuries, revived by métis with
an unmistakably unique signature. just as no flower
is perfectly proportioned, the métis demonstrate a
deliberate lack of symmetry, vibrant colours, sinuous
floral patterns, five-pointed stars, five-petaled flowers,
narrow linear leaves, twisted stems, small faceted
beads. the beadwork on vamps allows part of the
leather to show through. passed from grandmother or
mother, aunty or uncle to child, the art form was, and is
today, highly refined, reflecting the curvilinear patterns
of the eastern and western woodlands and prairies.
grandmothers and grandfathers, their daughters and
sons, wore cloth leggings, fringed with multiple silk
ribbons and intricate flowered embroidery and beading.

flowers themselves are star children. and star children
are daughters and sons of grandmother moon and
grandfather sun. they sleep all day, coming out to play

after dark when grandfather sun and grandmother moon are busy at their work. they can play any game, anywhere in the sky world, with only one rule. be home and in bed before dawn each day. not so hard to do you would think. but there was a night long ago when several star children took their games down to the treetops, skipping like stones across the waters. at first they were quiet. but soon enough their squeals of laughter woke a sister and brother. the earth kids couldn't help themselves. they put the star children into a panel bag. they wanted to keep them as pets.

panel bags are used to carry medicines, or flint and steel for starting fires in earlier times. depending on the skill in the beading or quillwork, embroidery or tufting, a panel bag could be traded for a horse. the high quality work, the beauty of the art forms, allows métis women and men to supplement, and even at times provide the family income. the breadth and variety of brightness of métis beadwork can be seen throughout turtle island. european-style clothing worn by indigenous peoples and whites alike, with floral quillwork, beadwork, silk embroidery, dyed horse or moose hair, shells, flossing and silk ribbon appliqué--all métis made. families and communities have distinctive beadwork styles and colours.

the families and communities of the star children would be angry, the star children thought. they worried they would be in trouble. all they did was fret, shining their lights inside the panel bag at night and crying throughout the day, homesick and lonely. the earth kids wanted them to play after dark, but the star children were too frightened. all they wanted was to go home. the earth kids wouldn't give in and the star children wouldn't come out of the panel bag to play. finally, on the fourth day, the earth kids felt so terrible they promised to let them go home. free at last, the star children played for many hours with the earth kids that night. while flying skyward with glee once again, they sang a song for the children and promised to send gifts to their new earth friends.

to be a métis beadworker, quilter, embroiderer, is a gift from the creator, from the star children. still complementing moccasins, coats, vests, belts, bags, barrettes, watches, necklaces, earrings, mittens, tablecloths, wall pockets, cloth frames for pictures, canvases, shawls, pow wow regalia, ceremonial clothing, sacred objects, and the list goes on, the effects of métis beadwork have spread throughout the world. historians and anthropologists seldom question the influence of father or son in indigenous

traditions, but with women's beadwork the familial connection is lost on the western mind. the arriving europeans' influence is given the credit for the quality and beauty achieved to this day. yet the women taught the art form for many hundreds of years before contact. investigation into methods of passing on these predominantly women's arts would reveal volumes.

the following day the girl and her brother, and every other earth child woke up to billions of brightly coloured plants--bees and other bugs to tend them. the earth kids picked flowers for their mothers, their fathers, their grandparents, their auntys and uncles, their friends. lovers gave each other flowers and artists painted them. the métis? why we embraced them in all of our art forms.

today, here is what one métis beadworker, barbra horsefall, has to say about beading: balance. beauty. challenge. dreams. following your intuition. connection to culture and community that came long before me. passing on teachings and a sense of peace, restfulness, onto the next generations. at the same time beading creates an excited feeling and an adrenaline rush. letting my ancestors guide my hand. figuring out how to do things with their help through dreams. beading is beauty through balance. once you discover that, you see everything in life has balance, relates to the whole world around you. that's my favorite part. the lesson of balance. it took me years to really discover and internalize that.

The house of learning

the acquisition of skills necessary for unearthing and then articulating meaning draws on knowledge from many areas, including oral tradition. curriculum delivery must take into account the requirements of the primary traditional learning modes of "experiential learning" and "learning by doing."

–joseph couture

fifteen years ago I was the only indigenous person in the english department at calgary's mount royal university. I have blue eyes and fair skin, long silver hair. I look like a white lady, so I blended in. didn't create discomfort among the staff. one year when the leaves were turning yellow and orange, a white, middle class person I knew from grad school congratulated me on my new sessional teaching job. we were lined up at the photocopy machine. I said I'd been teaching there a few years, mainstream and first peoples. the person took two steps back, pulling hands to belly in a kind of jittery dance. said, oh, you're teaching our native students here? I taught those people. be prepared to lower your expectations. to be disappointed with the level of their work. you won't last long. I didn't. no one does. me, I smiled and showed my imperfect teeth. I'm a métis, I said, and I love teaching there. the person swallowed hard, said, I'm so sorry to hear that, and bolted from the room.

not long after--right before he was made department chair--I heard a voice at my back. didn't catch him come in. his was a familiar rampage. proclaimed, natives' poverty is self-imposed. irresponsible with your government handouts. everyone has equal opportunity in this country. if you'd just accept your oppression as human beings. mankind is naturally aggressive and there will always be poor. there will always be racism. my parents and grandparents worked hard for what we have. anyone can. I turned to face him. I thought he was creating a swiftian satire. joking. but he was serious. revved. I didn't know what to say. told him my great uncle, harvey proulx, made a statue out of noxzema bottles at saint vincent's hospital in ottawa. the statue is still there.

growing up, my mother washed with noxzema. to this day, I love the smell. I've always associated noxzema with '60s tv and poverty. the poor woman's fancy face cream. I grew up in what today would be called a working poor family. the underclass. such lovely ways to refer to whole families--first peoples, métis, inuit, people of colour, whites. whole communities, whole villages, whose distrust of the wealthy who live off their backs is as honest as the sky is blue. these are the folks who're told all

their lives, from schools and teachers and books and tv, they don't belong. not in management, not in government, not in law, not in medicine, not in academia, not in university, not in a million years. less than a month later, I was fired--for my native-style teaching pedagogy.

near the end of that final term at mount royal university a woman in one of my indigenous students' courses spoke up in class to say that as a teacher, I was like nanabush, the trickster in tomson highway's the rez sisters. in the play, nanabush hardly speaks. even stage directions are sparse. s/he is a funny, clownish sort of character. teaches us what it is to live here on the planet earth. straddles the consciousness of the people and creator. this was the highest compliment I'd had as a teacher. I thought of a story an elderly métis guy once told me. he said it was a newer story, late 1500s, from the beginning times of the meetings of the europeans and the newly formed métis. to remind us if it's not possible to understand strange others, it is acceptable to move on. the story goes something like this: weasel's big brother, wolverine, decides to join a pack of dogs and wolves. his new companions treat him well, with care and kindness. teach him how to live comfortably in the pack. but wolverine is powerless to recognize valuable and important articles when they're pointed out to him, even after many tries. he misunderstands how the dogs and wolves store and preserve their food to supply them later on. as a result, wolverine constantly runs out of food. between that and his smaller size relative to the wolves and dogs, wolverine leaves the pack.

The strange others' house

first peoples did not enter intercultural encounters without expectations. they were already equipped with models of how dealings with familiar others worked, but for strange others they had to turn to other resources, those held in their story cycles.

—carla osborne

I recently heard of two tricksters travelling together, talking on and on about a good moose soup. one was ti-jean, métis trickster and big-hearted bungler. kind of like fire, that ti-jean, a creator and a destroyer. but then again, not like fire at all. the other trickster is san martin txiki, euskalkunak, all round stand up guy. even though they hadn't eaten in days, they were happy. they even kind of looked alike, skipped the same, winked the same, wore matching moccasins. ti-jean had a métis sash wrapped around his waist, flint tucked inside. txiki had a saw slung over his left shoulder. they reached the top of a sandy cliff, counted together, closed their eyes, and jumped.

txiki's people pursued their relatives whale and cod over great distances. had the technology for countless generations. reached the shores of turtle island seven, eight hundred years before the invaders planted their stakes and crosses in 1492. thousands of euskaldunak lived in newfoundland when cartier came looking for gold and riches. many more in labrador. new brunswick, québec. just as cartier and cabot reported seeing the euskaldunak, their whaling stations and fisheries, so the euskaldunak recorded seeing cabot and cartier. the euskaldunak peoples didn't make it into canada's history books till the 1970s. a good 1200 years after settling on canada's shores. why is that? because the euskaldunak had their own oral traditions? weren't considered civilized? because they're first peoples from parts of france and spain? maintain their culture and language to this day? because the first peoples of north america spoke basque to the french and spanish upon their arrival? because the first peoples of gaspé spoke a trade language that was half-basque?

face planted at the bottom of the cliff. the land here was different, thick forest, noticeably cooler. there was water not too far away, they could smell it, and they saw smoke peeking through the trees from a campfire. they brushed off the sand and without so much as a word they followed their empty bellies

hoping for a meal. the thought of food made them block out everything else—their manners, their good sense. ti-jean and txiki forgot to keep their true names to themselves. as soon as they reached the fire, they stood side by side and blurted out their names to some big giant fellow's bare back. turned his head around enough to show one ancient eye. a wihtikow. a man-eater. they knew they were doomed but it was too late for the friends to turn around and run. the wihtikow called them by name now, ordered them to gather firewood and roasting sticks. because he planned to eat those skinny critters for supper. boil em up. meat'll melt right off the bone. while carrying out the man-eater's orders, tricksters crossed paths with a weasel and asked for her help. weasel agreed to help her relatives.

is it because the euskaldunak call themselves by their own name? practice their matrilineal culture in their homeland until they're forced underground after the french revolution? because women hold key roles and places among their people? because they follow an oral history that includes a woman deity–– mari, and her lover, sugaar? because there are jentilak, giants and trickster and an oral history tens of thousands of years old? because euskaldunak have emigrated to many parts of the americas, joined with other cultures in large numbers and brought both their culture and language with them?

the man-eater was naked when tricksters met him in the trees that day. ti-jean and txiki saw a weakness there. they asked weasel to run up the wihtikow's anus and bite at his heart with her sharp little teeth. instant death. tricksters promised to rescue weasel from inside the man-eater's body. weasel agreed with their plan. went to work right away. wihtikow fell with skill and incredible speed, the hungry tricksters cut open the dead monster, pulled out weasel. revived her. they rewarded their tiny relative who saved their lives. gave her the gift of a new white coat with a striking black-tipped tail. the black tip was to honour weasel for her bravery till time immemorial. the two hungry tricksters continued their travels together, talking on and on about a good moose soup.